A Kid's Guide to Origami™

Making ORIGAMI FISH Step by Step

Michael G. LaFosse

The Rosen Publishing Group's
PowerKids Press™
New York

To "Evan" the fish

Published in 2002 by The Rosen Publishing Group, Inc.
29 East 21st Street, New York, NY 10010

First Edition

Book Design: Emily Muschinske
Project Editors: Jennifer Landau, Jason Moring, Jennifer Quasha

Illustration Credits: Michael G. LaFosse
Photographs by Cindy Reiman, background image of paper crane on each page © CORBIS.

LaFosse, Michael G.
Making origami fish step by step / Michael G. LaFosse.
    p. cm. — (A kid's guide to origami)
Includes bibliographical references and index.
  ISBN 0–8239–5873–6 (library binding)
1. Origami—Juvenile literature. [1. Origami. 2. Handicraft.] I. Title. II. Series.
  TT870 .L23396 2002
  736'.982–dc21
                                                                00–013047

Manufactured in the United States of America

Contents

What Is Origami?

Origami is the Japanese art of paper folding. In Japanese, "ori" means fold and "kami" means paper. People in Japan have enjoyed this art for hundreds of years. Today people all over the world practice origami. Like music, origami has a special language of **symbols**. No matter where you are from, the language of origami is the same. Once you learn these symbols, you can read an origami book from any country in the world.

All of the origami in this book is folded from square-shaped paper. Most origami paper only has color on one side, but you do not need to buy special origami paper. You can make origami using gift-wrapping paper, old magazines, colorful notepapers, even candy wrappers! Make sure that the paper is square and that it is the right size for your project. When you start a project, make sure that the origami paper faces the way the instructions suggest.

Some origami projects need more than one sheet

of paper. There are several of these **designs** in this book. By combining several folded shapes, you can make many kinds of decorations. The key on page 22 will help you make your origami projects. It also will help explain some of the terms, such as <u>mountain fold</u> and <u>valley fold</u>, that are used throughout the book.

Sea Star

Sea stars sometimes are called starfish even though they are not fish at all. They are closely related to sand dollars, sea urchins, and sea cucumbers. There are about 1,800 different kinds of sea stars and they come in all sizes and colors. They live both in shallow seas and in deep oceans. Most sea stars have five legs, but some kinds have many more.

You will need three sheets of the same size square paper to make a Sea Star. You can use tape while building the Sea Star, but if you fold it neatly you won't need to.

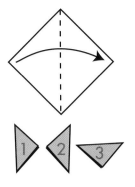

1

Fold pieces of paper in half, from one corner to the other corner, to make three triangles. If you are using origami paper, start with the white side up.

2

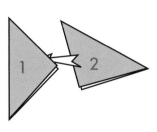

Fit two triangles together to make an arrow shape.

3

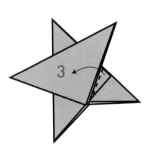

Place, or tape, the third triangle neatly on top of the arrow-shaped papers. Fold the little triangle-shaped paper from triangle number 1 over the top of triangle number 3. This will hold the third paper in place.

4

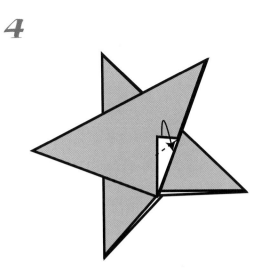

Fold the top corner of the little triangle over again to make a very small triangle.

5

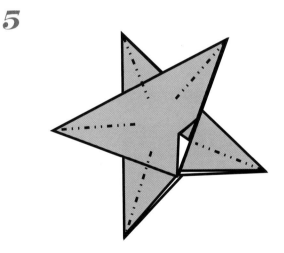

Use another square piece of paper. Fold the bottom corner to the top corner to make a triangle.

Sea Horse

The sea horse is an interesting fish. One reason is because the father sea horse, instead of the mother, gives birth to the babies! As soon as the babies are born, they quickly look for something, such as seaweed, to wrap their tails around. This helps the sea horse stay hidden and protected in the weeds. The sea horse's tail can grab like a monkey's tail!

First you can make a father Sea Horse from a big piece of paper. Then make a baby Sea Horse from a small piece of paper.

1

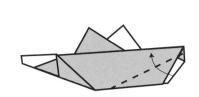

Begin with a square piece of paper. If you are using origami paper, start with the white side up. Fold the paper in half, leaving the two corners side by side like a cat's ears. These points will be the fins of the Sea Horse.

2

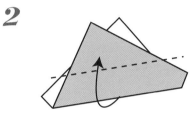

Bring up the bottom, folded edge close to the paper points that look like a cat's ears.

3

Fold up the left edge against the folded edge. Fold in the right edge to match the cut edge. Look ahead to drawing number four to see the shape.

4

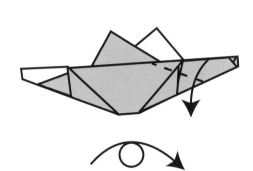

Fold up the right edge against the folded edge.

5

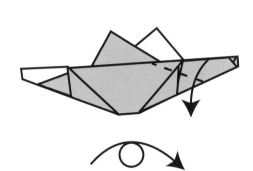

Fold down the right end of the paper. This is the tail. Turn the paper over so that it looks like drawing number six.

6

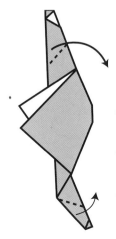

Fold down the top end to make the sea horse's head. Fold up the bottom end to finish the shape for the tail.

Stingray

Stingrays are a kind of fish. They are closely related to sharks, even though they look different. Most stingrays are very flat and diamond shaped. They like to live on the sea bottom in the sand, which they often use to hide themselves. Stingrays have a sharp spine at the base of their whiplike tails. They use this spine to protect themselves.

The skate is another flat fish that is closely related to the stingray. Skates look like stingrays but they do not have the stinging spine. One kind of skate protects itself with an electric shock, like the electric eel does.

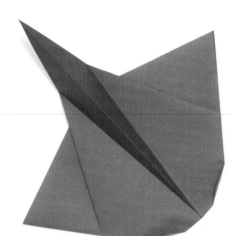

1

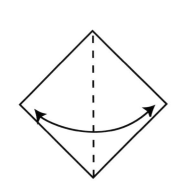

Begin with a square piece of paper. If you are using origami paper, start with the white side up. Fold the paper in half, from one corner to the other corner, and then unfold.

2

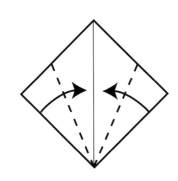

Fold up the two edges of the square to the crease, or fold, line.

3

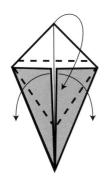

Fold out the two square corners to make the big fins of the Stingray. Fold down the top corner so that the point of the corner touches the center crease line.

4

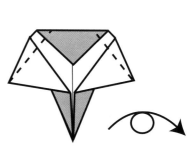

Fold in the two front edges of the fins to make a clean edge. Turn the paper over.

5

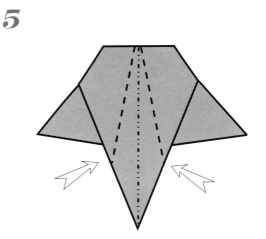

Make a <u>mountain fold</u> down the center of the tail. Add a <u>valley fold</u> to each side of the tail.

6

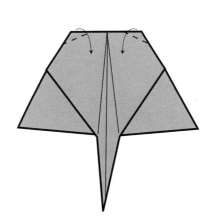

Fold down the two corners on the top to make the eyes.

Swordfish

The swordfish has a beautiful shape. This large animal lives in the open ocean, where it **preys** on schools of fish.

The origami Swordfish uses a cut. Even though many origami designs today do not use cutting, traditional Japanese paper folding does use cuts. In this project, pay special attention to the lettered corners. You can mark letters on your own paper to help learn how to fold the Swordfish.

1

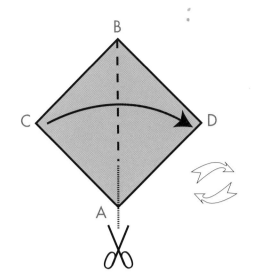

Begin with a square piece of paper. If you are using origami paper, start with the colored side up. Fold the paper in half, from one corner to the other corner, to make a triangle. Open the paper and cut a slit at the bottom, or corner A. Make the triangle again, and rotate it so that it looks like the triangle in drawing number two.

2

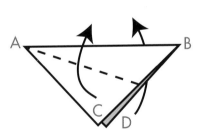

Now form the dorsal fin, or top fin, of the Swordfish. Fold up corners C and D above the top folded edge of the paper. C is folded in the front and D is folded to the back. Make sure to form a point at corner A, in the tail.

3

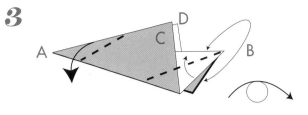

Fold down the front half of corner A to make the bottom half of the tail fin. Fold up the cut edges of corner B to match the folded edge. One cut edge folds up in front, and the other one in back. Turn the paper over so that it looks like drawing number four.

4

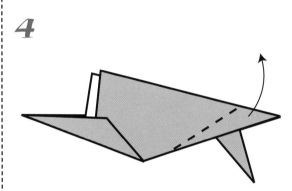

Fold up the top half of the tail fin. Look at drawing number five to see the shape.

5

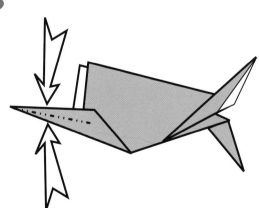

Pinch the "sword" of the swordfish flat to make it slender and pointy.

Fish

There are many kinds of fish. Fish come in all different shapes, sizes, and colors. Some fish live in the salty ocean and others live in freshwater lakes and streams.

In this project, try mixing different colors and sizes of paper. You can fold the paper many different ways to change the body, fins, and face of the fish. How many different kinds of fish can you make? You need two square pieces of paper to make one fish. Start with the same size paper, but later try mixing different sizes.

1

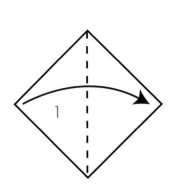

Fold the triangle in half. Unfold. Fold the other square in half, and then unfold. Fit the square into the triangle. Line up the creases so that they stay together.

2

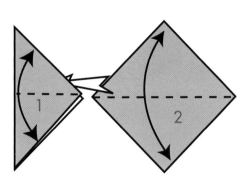

Fold the combined papers in half.

3

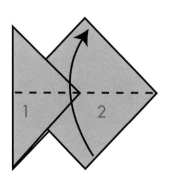

Fold down the front layers at an angle.

4

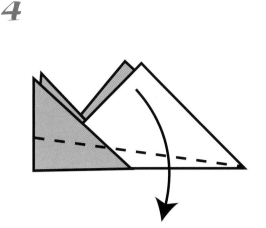

Make <u>mountain folds</u> and <u>valley folds</u> to the top and bottom two corners to make fins.

5

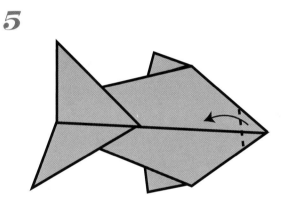

Fold over a small part of the front corner to make the fish's mouth.

6

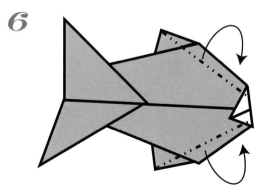

Mountain fold the top and bottom of the front edges.

Angelfish

Many people like angelfish because they are so beautiful. The origami Angelfish is a variation of the basic origami fish. How many kinds of Angelfish can you design? You will need two pieces of square paper to make one Angelfish. Start with the same size of papers, but later try mixing different sizes.

1

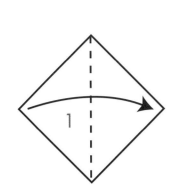

Begin with a square piece of paper. If you are using origami paper, start with the white side up. Fold both squares from one corner to the other corner to make triangles.

2

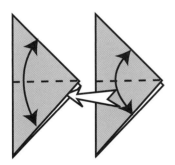

Fold the triangles in half again and unfold. Fit one triangle into the other, lining up the creases so that they stay together.

3

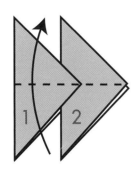

Fold the papers in half.

4

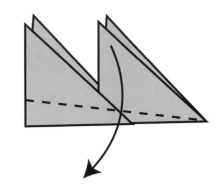

Fold the front layers down at an angle.

5

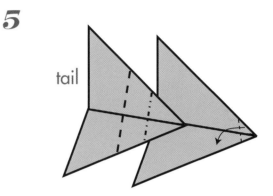

Make <u>mountain folds</u> and <u>valley folds</u> to the tail paper to make it shorter. Fold over a small part of the front corner to make the angelfish's mouth. Look at drawing number six to see the shape.

6

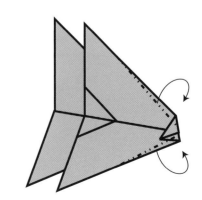

Mountain fold the front edges on the top, bottom, and over the back to make a clean shape.

Carp

Carp live in lakes, ponds, and streams. The fancy carp, called **koi**, are specially **bred** to have beautiful patterns of red and black. They can grow to be quite large, and most are kept in outdoor ponds. One of the most prized koi is called **Tancho Kohaku**. This fish is rare, has a single red spot on its white head, and can cost a lot of money, depending on its color patterns. This kind of koi reminds the Japanese of their country's flag, which is a red circle against a white background and which represents the rising sun. The koi fish is special to the Japanese.

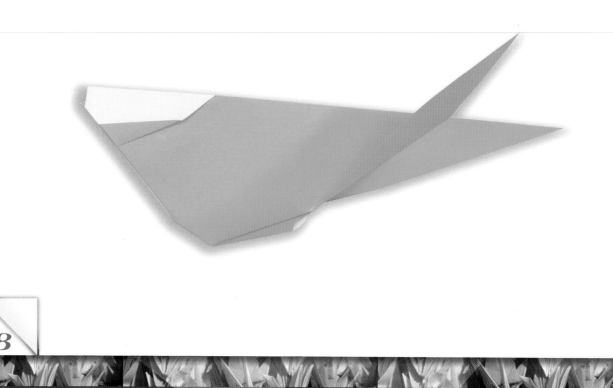

1

To make a Tancho Kohaku, you might want to use a square of origami paper that is red on one side and white on the other. Begin with the red side up. Fold in half from one corner to the other corner. Then unfold.

2

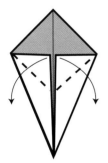

Fold two edges to the crease line.

3

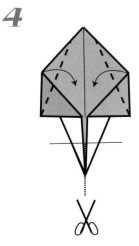

Fold out the two white square corners for the fins.

4

Cut a small slit at the bottom point where the tail will be. Fold in the top edges, but not all the way to the center. Look at drawing number five to see the shape.

5

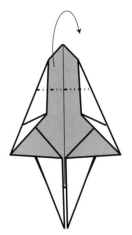

Mountain fold the top point to the back of the paper.

6

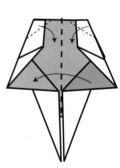

Fold in the top two corners. Then fold the paper in half up the middle.

7

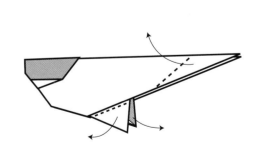

Position the paper to look like this. Fold up the front layer of the tail paper to make the tail fin. Fold out the other two fins on the belly to the sides. Give the tail a curve to make the fish look like it is swimming.

Shark

Sharks are **fascinating** and beautiful fish, even if they are scary. Sharks have no bones! Their skeleton is made of a tough, flexible material called **cartilage**. Unlike other fish, most sharks must keep swimming to breathe. They even swim while they sleep!

This origami shark is made of two pieces of paper so that you can make the mouth open and close. Steps one through five show how to make the **pectoral** fins, or fins on the chest area. You will need to fold a second piece of paper, following steps one through five of the Carp, to make the body and tail. When you put them both together, you have the Shark!

1

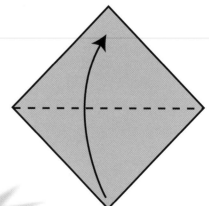

To make the front fins, begin with a square piece of paper. If you are using origami paper, start with the colored side up. Fold in half from one corner to the other corner to make a triangle.

2

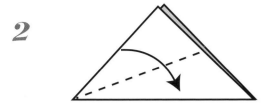

Fold down the top layer of the upper left edge to match the bottom folded edge of the triangle.

3

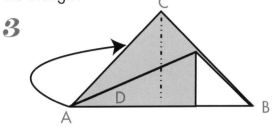

<u>Mountain fold</u> the left corner. Fold A around the back to match corner B.

4

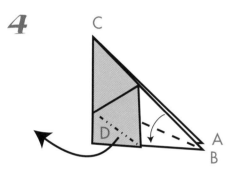

Pull out corner D to the left. Flatten. Notice how the white edge of the paper moves down to the bottom edge.

5

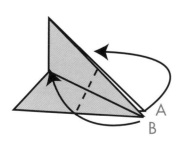

Now you have an arrow shape. This is what a great white shark's tooth looks like! Fold points B and A to touch the V-shaped notch between D and C. B goes to the front and A goes to the back.

6

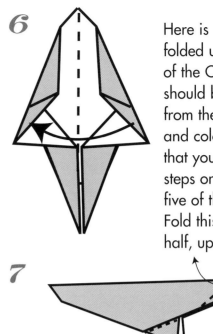

Here is a paper folded up to step five of the Carp. This should be folded from the same size and color of paper that you used for steps one through five of the Shark. Fold this shape in half, up the middle.

7

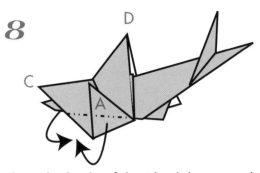

Fold up the front layer of the tail paper to shape the tail fin. Fold out the two fins on the belly to the sides.

8

Place the body of the Shark between the bent fins of the fin paper. Notice where C and D are. Fold the bottom corners of the fin paper inside the body of the Shark. This will lock them together.

9

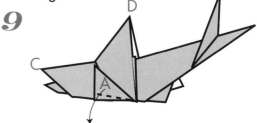

Fold down fins A and B. B is on the side you can't see. Move the tail up and down to open and close the mouth!

Origami Key

1. MOUNTAIN FOLD

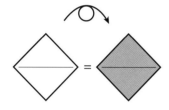

mountain fold line

To make a mountain fold, hold the paper so the white side is facing up. Fold the top corner back (away from you) to meet the bottom corner.

2. VALLEY FOLD

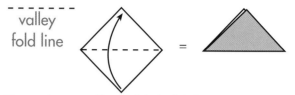

valley fold line

To make a valley fold, hold the paper so the white side is facing up. Fold the bottom corner up to meet the top corner.

3. TURN OVER

4. ROTATE

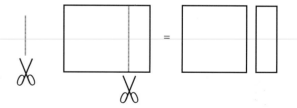

5. MOVE or PUSH

6. CUT

7. FOLD and UNFOLD

8. DIRECTION ARROW

Glossary

bred (BRED) Raised to produce special qualities.

cartilage (CAR-til-ij) A tough, flexible material in place of bone in an animal's skeleton. Your nose and your ears are formed of cartilage.

designs (dih-ZYNZ) Decorative patterns.

fascinating (FAS-in-ayt-ing) Very interesting.

koi (COY) A Japanese name for a kind of ornamental carp.

pectoral (PEK-tuh-ruhl) In the chest area.

preys (PRAYZ) Hunts other creatures for food.

symbols (SIM-bulz) Objects or designs that stand for something else.

Tancho Kohaku (TAHN-choh KOH-ha-koo) A Japanese name for a white koi with a single red spot on its head and no other markings.

Index

A
angelfish, 16

C
carp, 18
cartilage, 20
cutting, 12

E
electric eel, 10

J
Japan(ese), 4, 12, 18

K
koi, 18

M
mountain fold, 5

P
pectoral fins, 20

S
sea horse, 8
sea star, 6
sharks, 10, 20
skate, 10

skate, 10
stingray, 10
swordfish, 12

T
Tancho Kohaku, 18

V
valley fold, 5

Web Sites

Due to the changing nature of Internet links, PowerKids Press has developed an online list of Web sites related to the subject of this book. This site is updated regularly. Please use this link to access the list: www.powerkidslinks.com/kgo/maorfis/